W9-BWF-393

OCEANOGRAPHY LAB

~~DENNIS STRATTON CREMIN MEMORIAL~~
~~GAVIN NORTH SCHOOL~~
~~LAKE VILLA, ILLINOIS 60046~~

In Memoriam
Presented to

Dennis Stratton
Cremin Memorial
Learning Center

by

Naomi R. Scott
In Memory of

David Semple Scott

OCEANOGRAPHY LAB

SCIENTISTS AT WORK

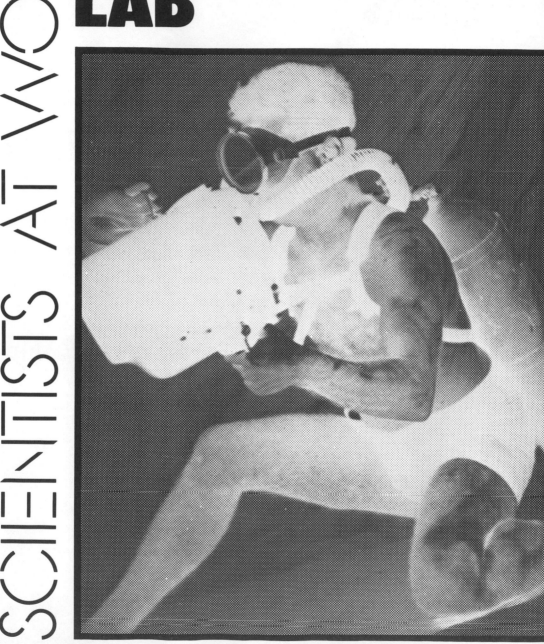

DENNIS STRATTON CREMIN MEMORIAL
GAVIN NORTH SCHOOL
LAKE VILLA, ILLINOIS 60046

MELVIN BERGER

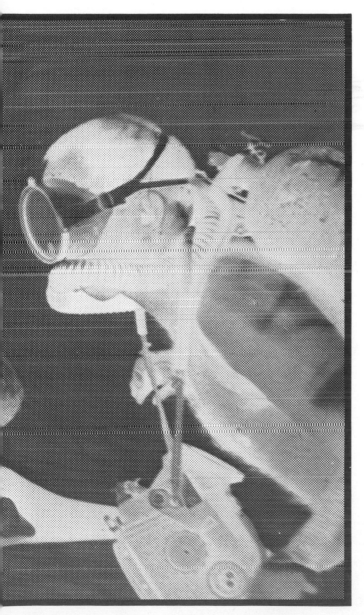

1,330N

THE JOHN DAY COMPANY
NEW YORK

OTHER TITLES IN THE SCIENTISTS AT WORK SERIES:
South Pole Station
The National Weather Service
Animal Hospital
Oceanography Lab
Pollution Lab
Cancer Lab
Consumer Protection Labs

Berger, Melvin.
     Oceanography lab.
     (His Scientists at work)
     SUMMARY: Discusses the daily activities of oceanographers at the Woods Hole Ocean-
ographic Institution and some of the current problems in oceanographic research.
     1. Oceanographers—Juvenile literature. 2. Woods Hole, Mass. Oceanographic Institute
—Juvenile literature. [1. Oceanographers. 2. Woods Hole, Mass. Oceanographic Institute]
I. Title.
GC30.A1B4   551.4'6   72-2417
ISBN: 0-381-99940-8 RB

Copyright © 1973 by Melvin Berger

All rights reserved. No part of this book may be reprinted, or reproduced or utilized in any
form or by any electronic, mechanical or other means, now known or hereafter invented,
including photocopying and recording, or in any information storage and retrieval system,
without permission in writing from the Publisher.

Published in Canada by Fitzhenry & Whiteside Limited, Toronto.

Printed in the United States of America

3   4   5   6   7   8   9   10

For Vivienne Hochman,
whose house on Cape Cod was my home
during the writing of this book.

CONTENTS

DENNIS STRATTON CREMIN MEMORIAL
GAVIN NORTH SCHOOL
LAKE VILLA, ILLINOIS 60046

ACKNOWLEDGMENTS

I am very grateful to Mr. John L. Schilling, Public Information Officer of the Woods Hole Oceanographic Institution, for arranging my visits to the Institution, for our long hours of conversation, for furnishing me with much research material, and for reading through the finished manuscript. Mr. Clyde L. MacKenzie, Jr., of the National Marine Fisheries Service Laboratory at Milford, Connecticut, gave me valued information on fish farming, and Dr. Holger W. Jannasch, of the Woods Hole Oceanographic Institution, and Dr. Kenneth Gold, of the Osborn Marine Laboratories, were very kind in providing information on their special fields of activity and in checking over parts of the manuscript. My thanks, finally, to the wonderful men and women at the Woods Hole Oceanographic Institution who were so hospitable and made me feel so very welcome during my many visits.

FOREWORD

What mysterious force is it that turns man's attention to the sea? Is it that we have evolved from the sea? Is it the challenge of the unknown? Are we trying to punish ourselves with the sea's cruelness? Just what is it?

The sea is both beautiful and ugly, peaceful and full of rage, helpful and destructive. But it has always held a charm for man, who seeks answers to endless questions.

The sea has always been needed and used by man, first in only a limited way but gradually expanding to all corners of the earth. Explorers have had the desire to know just what was over the horizon, what new land could be found, and what new adventure awaited. This need has driven man to go to the tropics, to the poles, into raging storms, spend long days without the comforts of home and, yes, even to his death. All of this to learn more about the sea.

Today, young men and women are still enduring these things, but in a different way. The adventure and challenge of the sea is still there. But the needs have changed. Now they look at the entire sea—water, bottom, animals, nutrients, currents, pollution, minerals and weather.

They ask new questions: Are we slowly killing the sea? Will man live in the sea and work on the ocean floor? Can we control our weather? How do we feed the world? What drugs are in the sea?

We still do not have the answers. But today scientists are working on these questions in oceanography labs, such as the Woods Hole Oceanographic Institution. They are using the latest scientific equipment to unlock the mysteries of the sea.

JOHN L. SCHILLING
Public Information Officer
Woods Hole Oceanographic Institution

OCEANOGRAPHY LAB

OCEANS AND OCEANOGRAPHERS

The oceans of the world are wide and vast. More than 70 percent of our planet is under water.

And the oceans are amazingly deep. In one spot it is nearly seven miles from the surface to the ocean bottom. Over all, the oceans have an average depth of more than two miles.

These enormous bodies of water throb with life. Thousands of different types of plants and animals grow in the sea. More than 90 percent of all plant life in the world is found here. There are sea plants so tiny that they can be seen only through a powerful microscope. On the other hand, a kind of seaweed called kelp is

Oceanographers at work.

National Oceanic and Atmospheric Administration (NOAA)

the largest plant on earth. It grows even taller than the immense redwoods of California.

The fish and other sea animals also come in every size you could imagine. The largest mammal known to man, the blue whale, lives in the sea. A full-grown blue whale can be 100 feet long and weigh 300,000 pounds!

Some people think that the ocean floor is flat and smooth. The very opposite is true. It is rough and rugged. Both giant mountains and deep valleys are found beneath the sea. One valley beneath the Pacific Ocean is deep enough to hold Mt. Everest, the tallest mountain on earth!

Man has always been curious about the oceans. But it was only about one hundred years ago, in 1872, that scientists began to study the ocean. In that year, the British ship H.M.S. *Challenger* set sail for a three-and-one-half-year scientific cruise. This voyage marked the birth of the science of the sea, or oceanography. It also gave rise to the most fascinating sea creatures, the men and women who study the sea, the oceanographers.

Oceanographers today are a very special kind of people. Most started their studies in one of the major fields of science—biology, chemistry, geology, or whatever. But along with their interest in science they also had a strong interest in the sea. During their advanced studies they combined their science with their love of the sea. The biologist learned about life in the ocean. The chemist learned about the chemical elements found in sea water. The geologist learned about the ocean bottom. And so on.

The oceanographers find the sea a challenging field for research. The sea does not give up its secrets easily. It is always changing and always moving. It batters their ships; it destroys their tools.

NOAA

Oceanographers taking underwater photographs.

And unless they have very strong stomachs, it also gives them long periods of seasickness.

But oceanographers are dedicated to their chosen field of science. They do not agree with the English writer Samuel Johnson, who once said: "No man will go to sea who has the wit to get himself into jail. And in jail, the food is better and the company just as good."

Oceanographers consider the study of the sea the most rewarding, satisfying and important of all scientific activities.

WOODS HOLE OCEANOGRAPHIC INSTITUTION

Oceanographers sail over every ocean on the face of the globe to do their research. They sail from oceanography laboratories located throughout the world. One of the most outstanding of these laboratories is located on the eastern coast of the United States. It is the Woods Hole Oceanographic Institution.

Woods Hole is a small village on Cape Cod. The Cape is a narrow strip of land that curls out into the Atlantic Ocean, just south of Boston, Massachusetts. During the last century Woods Hole was famous as a port for whaling ships. Today it is famous as the home of the Woods Hole Oceanographic Institution.

In 1930 the National Academy of Sciences chose Woods Hole as the ideal site for a new oceanography laboratory. It has an excellent deep-water harbor. It is only about 200 miles to the important Gulf Stream. And Cape Cod is a natural boundary between the cold water and sea life of the Grand Banks off Newfoundland and the warm water and sea life of Florida.

Woods Hole Oceanographic Institution is a very long name, even for this large and important laboratory. The scientists working here have shortened the name in various ways. Sometimes they just use the initials, WHOI, and pronounce it Hooey. Other times they call it the Oceanographic. Perhaps the most popular name is the Institution. Oceanographers all over the world know that the Institution means the Woods Hole Oceanographic Institution.

The Institution brings together about 150 highly trained scientists, men and women, who do research on the oceans of the world. The scientists are backed up by some 450 assistants, technicians, secretaries and other helpers.

The scientists work in three large buildings that are crowded with laboratories and offices. The laboratory buildings are clustered around the Institution's dock area. Here the four ocean-going research ships and the one research submarine tie up between cruises.

At any one moment perhaps one hundred of the scientists are at work in their shore laboratories. The others may be out on scientific cruises. Some will be sailing through the Black Sea, studying the chemistry of the water. Another group may be collecting fish in the water near the Arctic Circle. The third ship may be in the Indian Ocean, digging up mud samples from the ocean bottom. And the remaining ship may be sailing along the coast of South America, as the scientists prepare a new map of the continental

A view of the labs and ships of the Woods Hole Oceanographic Institution

shelf. One or two scientists may be out in the research submarine, photographing and collecting objects of interest on the sea floor.

Oceanographers divide their time between their shore and ship laboratories. Some men and women spend many months each year at sea. Others go to sea for just a short time each year. They do most of their work in the shore laboratories. Each scientist chooses the most valuable way to spend his time.

STARTING A RESEARCH PROJECT

Ask any oceanographer at the Institution how he started his research project. He will often begin by saying, "I was interested in learning more about..." Then he will go on to describe his work.

Every year more than two hundred separate research studies are pursued at the Institution. A recent list ranges from Number 1: A Study of Fish in the North Atlantic, to Number 206: Safety Research.

Some oceanographers are interested in collecting basic facts and figures about the ocean. They measure the chemical content of sea water, map the ocean floor, study the life patterns of fish, and so on. They choose projects that will increase the foundation of knowledge upon which the science of oceanography rests.

Other oceanographers choose projects that will have practical uses. They develop improved methods of catching fish, examine what happens to sewage dumped into the ocean, observe the effect of sewage on sea life, and in various ways help government agencies, business firms and others who use the ocean.

Once he has chosen a research topic, the oceanographer talks about it with other scientists. During coffee breaks and in informal chats, he describes his idea to them. They tell him what they think of it and make suggestions.

If it still seems like a good idea, the scientist goes over the proposal with the chairman of his department. The Institution is divided into five departments: biology (life in the sea), chemistry (chemicals in the sea), geology (the bottom and edges of the sea), physical oceanography (ocean currents), and ocean engineering (research tools and instruments). The chairman of each department is an experienced scientist and is able to offer valuable advice.

Approval from the chairman means that the scientist may present his plan at a meeting with scientists from other departments. The other scientists discuss the idea. They raise questions that may not have occurred to members of the same department.

An outsider at one of these meetings might think the criticisms harsh and nasty. A scientist's best friend may attack parts of his proposal. But his purpose is to improve the project. After the meeting they are still close friends.

Some projects do not survive these close examinations. They are

Several scientists get together
to talk over a chart
made of the ocean bottom.

WHOI

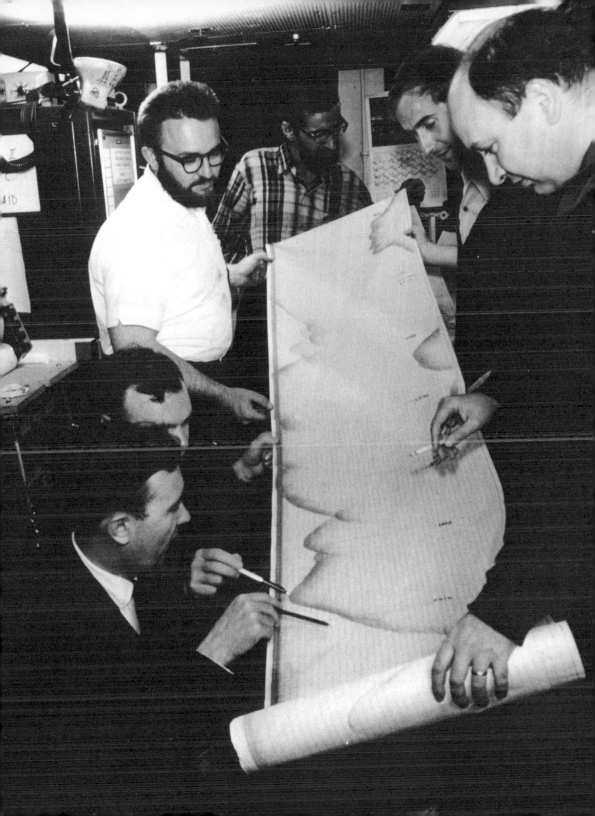

dropped. Other projects convince everyone of their value. Then the scientist goes ahead.

His first problem is to find the money to pay for the research. The Institution has a budget of about $10 million a year. A small part of this comes from gifts to the Institution or from private industry. Almost the entire amount—about 95 percent—comes from various government agencies. The scientist usually applies to a government agency for a grant of money to cover the cost of his research.

He writes up a description of the purpose, methods and expected results of his project. He lists the supplies, helpers, laboratory space and ship time that he will need. Then he sends the proposal to the government agency that he thinks will be most interested.

Each government office has committees of scientists who carefully study the proposals it receives. Since only limited funds are available, only the most worthwhile projects are chosen. The committees ask themselves: Will this study add to the science of oceanography? Is it good science? Is this scientist the best person to do the research?

Most of the proposals sent out by scientists at the Institution are approved. If a proposal is rejected, the Institution helps the unlucky scientist to rework his application. It is sent to another agency. However, if the scientist does not get funds soon, the Institution is forced to let him go.

Many scientists complain about this way of paying for research. They feel that they spend too much time applying for funds. They lack freedom in choosing their research projects. Often they pick a subject that they know will interest a particular agency in order to be sure of getting a grant.

Although there are things wrong with this system of obtaining funds to start a research project, the fact is that it works. The proof is that many very remarkable discoveries have come out of the Institution.

AT WORK IN THE SHORE LABORATORIES

The oceanographers arrive for work at the Woods Hole Oceanographic Institution around 8 o'clock in the morning. At a glance they look like tourists or visitors to Woods Hole. They are dressed informally—shorts and polo shirts in the summer, slacks and sweaters in the colder weather. Many of the men have beards.

Probably the easiest way to recognize a scientist is by his lunch bag. There is no cafeteria at the Institution. Most of the scientists bring their own lunches. Sometimes they refer to each other as "Brown Baggers."

Inside the buildings, the scientists head for their laboratories.

M. Berger

Tangles of wires connect the different parts of a computer.

Most laboratories are rather small rooms, crowded with scientific equipment, desks and books.

No two laboratories look alike. The type of research and the type of person using the laboratory determine its appearance.

In one lab an entire wall is covered with a complicated maze of glass tubes filled with bubbling colored liquids. The large desks and walls of another room are covered with maps and charts that show features of the ocean floor. And the shelves in still another laboratory are lined with glass bottles containing preserved sea animals or plants.

There is a room at the Institution crowded with the gray metal cabinets that contain a large, powerful computer. A tangle of wires connects the components.

Although each laboratory is unique, they all have one feature in common—the coffee pot. It is said that there are more coffee pots than microscopes in the Institution!

The coffee is more important to the science of oceanography than you might think. Advances in modern oceanography are seldom made by one scientist working alone. Most discoveries come from the combined efforts and thoughts of many researchers. And it is frequently over a cup of coffee that oceanographers exchange information and new ideas.

Scientists also talk during weekly lunch-time get-togethers. Since everyone munches his sandwich at these meetings, they are called the gatherings of the Peanut Butter Club. Each week there is a different program. One week a scientist shows slides from a recent cruise; another time a scientist reports on an interesting research finding; the following week someone tells about a meeting he attended, and so on.

A stroll through the halls of the Institution reveals scientists engaged in all sorts of activities. Many are at work at their laboratory benches—bent over a microscope, mixing chemicals in a beaker, adjusting dials on an electronic instrument, picking tiny bits out of a mud sample, or building a new tool.

Several scientists are seated at their desks. Desk work is an important part of oceanography. The scientists write up proposals

An instrument is carefully tested
in the shore laboratory
before being taken to sea.

NOAA

for new grants. They keep records of their experiments. And they prepare reports of completed research projects.

Part of their desk time is spent in reading. Every month reports on research in oceanography appear in magazines, called journals. To keep up with the advances in oceanography the scientists read a few of these journals every month. They also read the important new books in their fields.

Every now and then you look into a laboratory room and discover that it is deserted. There are no scientists to be seen anywhere.

Most likely these "missing" scientists are on one of the ships or submarines of the Institution. They are doing research at sea. For many oceanographers, going to sea is the most exciting part of their work.

SETTING SAIL

The dock at the Woods Hole Oceanographic Institution is crowded and busy whenever a research cruise is about to depart. As many as twenty-five scientists leave at one time on a trip that might last over a year.

We can watch twenty scientists prepare for a ten-day cruise to the North Atlantic Ocean.

The scientists begin to arrive at the dock a few hours before sailing time. Most carry heavy suitcases with the clothes they will wear at sea. Several friends and relatives accompany each of the scientists.

Tied up alongside the dock is their ship, the R/V *Knorr*, the

Research Vessel *Knorr*. The majestic Knorr has a dark blue hull, with a shiny white superstructure up above. It is one of the newest and most modern vessels built for scientific research. The four laboratories on board are equipped like the finest shore laboratories.

The ship's crew and workers from the laboratory help the scientists carry their special equipment and supplies aboard. They range from clumsy, heavy tools to delicate, sensitive electronic instruments.

Most of the attention centers around the chief scientist. For this cruise the chief scientist is a marine chemist. His research project is to collect some special samples of sea water. He will study the chemical content of these samples. He will be searching

Scientists bring their equipment onto the KNORR.

M. Berger

M. Berger

*A laser that will
be used for
underwater experiments.*

for tiny amounts of certain chemical elements that might be dissolved in the water.

Plans for this trip began a full year ago. At that time the chemist put forth his proposal to the Institution's Ship Committee. This committee plans the schedule of cruises for the four ships of the Institution.

The committee approved his proposal. Together they worked out the dates for the cruise. (There is an old tradition in oceanography that cruises never start on a Friday. Ships from the Institution leave on any other day of the week—but never on Friday.)

The chemist planned all the details of the cruise. He mapped the route of the *Knorr*. He chose the scientists who would help him.

M. Berger

Supplies and equipment are brought together on the deck of the KNORR.

He prepared a list of the laboratory space, the supplies and equipment he needed.

The chief scientist did not need all the room on the *Knorr*. Therefore, he approached other scientists to offer them the empty space. A few scientists who were able to fit their research needs in with his plans also agreed to go along.

One scientist will experiment with shining a laser beam through sea water. He wants to see how much light is blocked by fish or other forms of sea life. He will collect biological samples at the same point. His hope is to develop the laser beam into an oceano-graphic research tool.

Another scientist brings on board several types of underwater measuring tools. They will measure the temperature, saltiness or salinity, speed of movement, and weight of the water at different places and depths.

One group of scientists is planning to study the amount of radioactivity in the water. They will draw up water while the ship is steaming. A machine on the *Knorr* will automatically measure any radioactivity in the water.

The scientists and their helpers rush to load the ship quickly. Every once in a while a scientist discovers that he has forgotten some necessary tool or supply. He dashes from the ship to his laboratory to get the missing item. An entire experiment may be ruined if a wire or filter or battery is forgotten.

Some supplies do not arrive until the very last minute. Just one half hour before sailing time a laundry truck arrives on the dock bringing clean towels and sheets. Minutes later another truck pulls up with fresh fruit and vegetables. The ship's crew quickly get these supplies on board.

Suddenly there is a deafening blast of the *Knorr*'s powerful whistle. The loud sound startles the people on the dock. It is a signal that the *Knorr* is about to sail. Husbands, wives, children and friends of the scientists and crew members exchange a last hug and kiss. Other workers and scientists who have come to the dock from the laboratories shake hands and wave. Everyone is excited to witness the beginning of a voyage.

There are two more blasts of the *Knorr*'s loud whistle. Two young men throw over the ropes that hold the *Knorr* to the dock.

In a moment the proud, graceful ship backs out and away from Woods Hole. Silently she turns and heads toward the open sea.

The scientists, hot and tired after loading the boat, line the rail. They wave and shout good-byes to their well-wishers on the dock.

The KNORR *glides silently through the water— off on a cruise for science.*

M. Berger

The ship glides along rapidly, and their friends are soon out of sight.

Their thoughts turn to the sea, and to the adventures awaiting them on this cruise for science.

AT WORK ON THE SHIP

As soon as the *Knorr* is out of Woods Hole harbor, the scientists take a close look at the ship that will be both their home and their laboratory for the next ten days.

The *Knorr* is a new and comfortable ship. Every inch of space is put to use. The scientists sleep two to a room, on bunk beds. The rooms are tight and compact. Each one has just enough room for the beds, a dresser, a closet and a desk.

The halls between the rooms are narrow. The mess hall, where the scientists eat, and the combination lounge and library are light, pleasant rooms. But again one feels that there is no wasted space.

NOAA

*The wire cable that is used
to lower equipment into the water.*

The four laboratories on the *Knorr* are larger than the typical laboratories on shore. They must be big enough to hold the special equipment that is placed in the labs for each cruise. On one trip a laboratory may be filled with apparatus to measure the amounts of the chemicals in sea water. The very next time out the same laboratory may contain tanks to keep large fishes alive for the trip back to Woods Hole.

The scientists who have been on cruises before relax during the first few hours at sea. They know that soon they will be busy with a full heavy schedule of scientific activities.

A typical day starts at dawn. After being awakened, the scientist has a quick breakfast and climbs up to the outside deck. He fills his lungs with the fresh, salty sea air. The wind musses his hair as he gets ready for the day's work.

Bringing a large sample of water on board is hard work.

NOAA

In a little while the ship will stop in mid-ocean. It will stay in one spot for a few hours. This is called a station. Many experiments can be done only at a station.

The scientist who will be doing an experiment at the next station prepares all of his equipment in advance. He must be ready to start the instant the ship stops. It costs about $4,000 a day to run the *Knorr*. Every minute is valuable.

Most of the experiments done at a station use a heavy wire cable to lower some instrument or tool into the water. The chief

It is difficult to do delicate experiments on a rocking ship.

WHOI

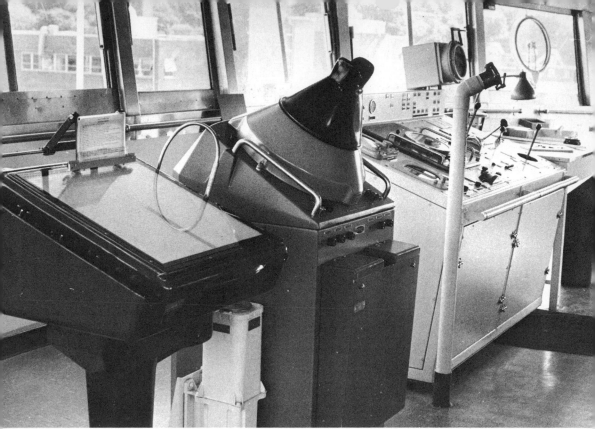

M. Berger

The modern navigational equipment on the bridge of the KNORR.
The oceanographers stand watch here.

scientist uses his time on the wire to fill containers with water from certain depths. The other scientists use their wire time to lower the laser and to place measuring tools in the water.

Lowering equipment on the wire can be hard work. And it is almost never done without running into some sort of trouble. Over and over again equipment that worked perfectly during all its tests stops working when it is put to actual use.

Between stations, many scientists work in the ship's laboratories. This work is not easy either. One oceanographer guesses that he works only half as well at sea as he does in his shore laboratory. Although the *Knorr* is a smooth-sailing ship, it rocks and sways in the sea. A careful examination through a microscope or a delicate chemical test becomes very difficult when you must brace yourself to keep from falling.

The oceanographers also take turns in standing instrument watch. They go up to the bridge, where the *Knorr*'s captain directs the running of the ship, for four hours on duty. During that time they keep a check on the various scientific instruments that are collecting information from the water.

At the first warning of a storm, the scientists are asked to help the crew, and serve extra time on look-out. Seamanship is not part of the college courses in oceanography. But many oceanographers are first-rate sailors as well as scientists. During a storm or other emergency, some scientists may go for thirty-six hours without sleep.

In case of fire, collision or man overboard, each scientist goes to his special duty station. He has some tasks to perform there. Everyone on board, scientist and crew member, follows the captain's orders to avoid any injuries or damage.

If it has been a quiet day, the oceanographers try to get together from four to five o'clock in the afternoon for a "Happy Hour." They talk about the day's work. They make plans for the next day. They chat about the weather and the sea. They swap stories about other scientists and other cruises.

After the Happy Hour, it is chow time—the Navy word for time to eat. The men enjoy the good filling meal prepared by the chef on the *Knorr*.

When chow is over, the scientists get back to work—in their laboratory, standing watch, writing up a report, studying or reading. A few sit down in the lounge for a game of bridge or cribbage. These are the favorite games of sea-going oceanographers.

As the evening wears on, the scientists head for their cabins one by one. A day at sea is a long day, and no one knows what the next day will bring.

There is always some work to be done in the ship's laboratories.

NOAA

RESEARCH SUBMARINE *ALVIN*

Groups of scientists from the Woods Hole Oceanographic Institution sail over the seven seas in research ships. At the same time one or two scientists crawl along the ocean floor in the Institution's tiny research submarine, *Alvin*.

The *Alvin* is much smaller than a Navy submarine. It is only 22 feet long and weighs 16 tons. The heart of the *Alvin* is a seven-foot-round sphere made of high-strength steel over one inch thick. A pilot and one or two scientists can barely squeeze into the tiny sphere.

The *Alvin* must be transported to the spot where it will dive. It can go down to depths of over a mile. Beneath the water, the

Alvin can move at speeds as high as three knots. It can remain underwater up to sixteen hours.

The *Alvin* has three propellers to move it in all directions through the water. The power is provided by three large groups of batteries. In the event of an accident or emergency the heavy batteries are dropped. Large tanks of mercury used to balance the *Alvin* are also dumped. The *Alvin* then floats up to the surface.

The scientists inside the *Alvin* can look through four portholes

The research submarine ALVIN *about to be lowered into the water.*

WHOI

to see ahead, to the sides, and beneath the submarine. They control the powerful mechanical arm that juts out from the front of the submarine. Whenever a scientist sees an object of interest in the ocean, he grasps it with the mechanical arm and places it in a tray that is attached to the hull of the *Alvin*.

The *Alvin* is equipped with both movie and still cameras. It also has the powerful lights necessary to take pictures in the darkness of the ocean depths. A tape recorder makes it possible to record the sounds heard on the floor of the ocean.

The ALVIN's *mechanical arm and tray to hold samples.*

WHOI

Ever since it was built, in 1964, the oceanographers at the Institution have put the *Alvin* to good scientific use. One discovery made with the *Alvin* cleared up a mystery that had bothered oceanographers for a long time.

Oceanographers measure the ocean depth by bouncing a sound off the bottom and recording how long it takes for the echo to return. Sometimes, though, during experiments the echo came back too soon. It seemed impossible for the water to be that shallow. One explanation was that there might be schools of fishes at

A view inside the crowded passenger sphere of the ALVIN.

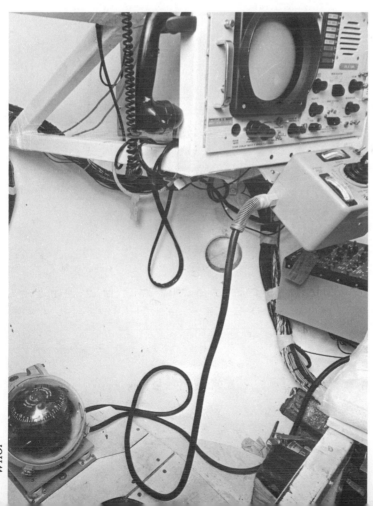

WHOI

the higher level. The sound was bouncing off this layer of fish, rather than the bottom of the sea. But no one could prove that there was a fish layer.

The *Alvin* was used to test the theory. A few miles off Woods Hole, the *Alvin* dived down to the suspected level of fish. It stopped, dark and silent.

Suddenly the scientists flashed on the lights. They saw that the submarine was surrounded by thousands and thousands of fish. A net attached to the mechanical arm was used to capture several of the fish for further study.

This dive of the *Alvin* proved that it was a layer of fish that gave the false depth readings. And the fish samples showed the kinds of fish that produced the echoes.

The *Alvin* has become the pet of the scientists at the Institution. Partly it is because the *Alvin* is such a valuable research tool. But more than that, the *Alvin* has won a special place in everyone's heart because of the amazing adventures it has had.

Early in 1966 a United States bomber accidentally dropped an H-bomb in the ocean off the coast of Spain. The *Alvin* was flown to Spain to help in the recovery operation. After about twelve days of diving, the pilot of the *Alvin* found a track made by the bomb as it slipped down the sharply-sloped ocean bottom. They followed the track to the bomb itself. The bomb lay entangled in the lines of the parachute to which it was attached.

There were a few bad moments when the *Alvin* also got caught by the parachute ropes. There was a danger, too, that the tiny submarine would start an avalanche of mud that would swamp the vessel.

After being located by the *Alvin*, the H-bomb was finally recovered. Overnight, the *Alvin* became famous throughout the world.

The *Alvin* was brought back to the United States. It was overhauled and repaired. In the summer of 1967 it was returned to service.

Soon afterwards the *Alvin* was on a dive off the coast of South Carolina. The pilot noticed a black "rock" six feet long, in front of the submarine. Suddenly, the "rock" came to life. It charged at the *Alvin* at high speed. Too late to move the submarine, the men inside felt the whole ship shake as a 200-pound swordfish rammed it with his sharp, powerful sword. The fish's sword became tightly wedged into one of the *Alvin*'s seams.

The 200-pound swordfish that attacked the ALVIN.

WHOI

The *Alvin*—with the swordfish still attached—was brought to the surface. The fish was removed. The *Alvin* was examined and found to have suffered no damage. And the cook prepared a delicious swordfish-steak dinner that evening.

Great care is taken when lowering or raising the ALVIN.

WHOI

The adventures of the *Alvin* continued. One day it was being hauled out of the water when the wires got tangled, and the submarine's mechanical arm was knocked off. It sank in nearly one mile of water. Could the *Alvin* recover the small arm? Or would

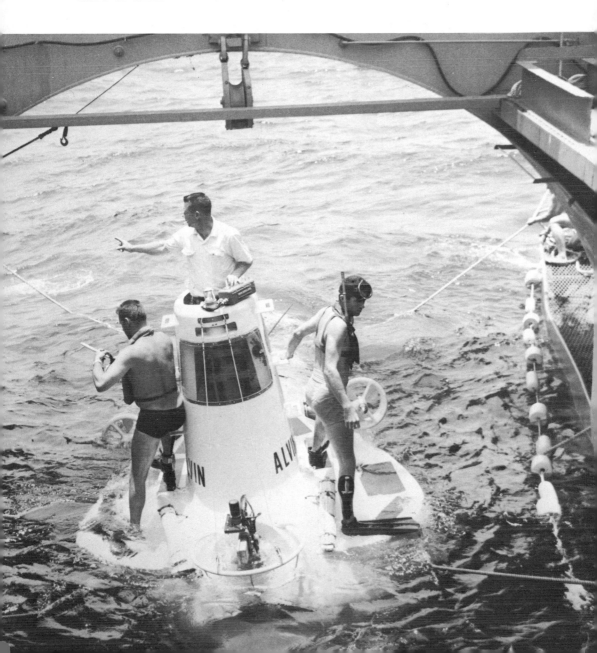

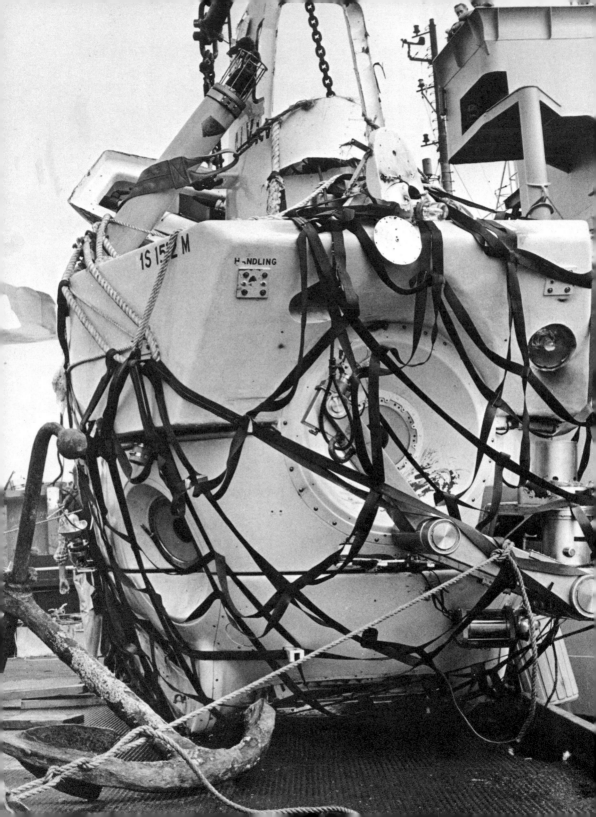

it be necessary to build and attach a new arm, at a cost of about $50,000?

By now, you must realize that all *Alvin* stories have happy endings. This one is no exception. The crew of the *Alvin* located the arm and photographed it lying on the ocean floor. In another dive they recovered the missing piece. Later it was attached to the *Alvin* at a cost of less than $5,000.

In October, 1968, the *Alvin* was towed for a dive about 135 miles south of Woods Hole. All at once, the heavy wire holding the *Alvin* broke. The empty submarine plunged into the water. It quickly sank out of sight. It came to rest at the bottom of the ocean, about one mile beneath the surface.

The following summer, a team of Navy ships and submarines was brought together to try to raise the *Alvin*. With a great deal of difficulty, one of the submarines was able to attach a line to the *Alvin*. A large ship on the surface hauled up the *Alvin* and placed it on a barge. On September 1, 1969, the *Alvin* was safely back on the dock of the Institution.

The *Alvin* had again made oceanographic history. It is the largest object recovered from the greatest depth in the history of ocean engineering. The scientists learned much about the difficulties of rescuing a submarine and about the sea itself. But perhaps the most fascinating discoveries came from examining the lunch box that had been submerged in the *Alvin* for over ten months.

The ALVIN *is raised*
after sitting on the ocean bottom
for ten months.

WHOI

BACTERIA IN THE SEA

Dr. Holger W. Jannasch of the Woods Hole Oceanographic Institution was curious to examine the food that had been in the *Alvin*. The pilot had packed a baloney sandwich, a thermos jug of beef broth and an apple for lunch. He had put the plastic lunch box on board the *Alvin*. But before he had entered the submarine, the lines holding the *Alvin* had broken and it sank.

The lunch box was not watertight, and the thermos cracked under the high pressure of the water at a depth of nearly one mile. Sea water flooded everything. For ten months the food soaked in water on the ocean floor.

Dr. Jannasch is a marine biologist studying the germs, or bac-

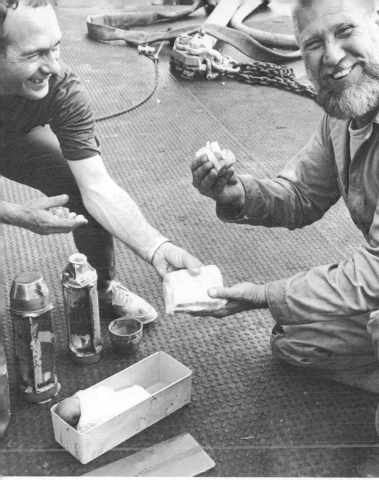

*Do you want a bite?
Hope you don't
mind that it has been
soaking in sea
water for nearly a year.*

WHOI

teria, that grow in the sea. He expected that the food would be completely spoiled by the bacteria that were on it to begin with, as well as by the bacteria in the water, and that the food would be smelly and not fit to be eaten. In fact, the whole idea of dumping sewage and garbage into the ocean is based on the belief that it will be decomposed by bacteria.

To his amazement, the food was in excellent condition. The baloney, although grayish on the outside, could still be eaten. The broth was saltier than usual, but otherwise was perfect. The apple had a pickled appearance, but was still firm and solid, and could be eaten safely.

What had happened?

Dr. Jannasch decided to investigate. First he checked over the *Alvin*. Perhaps acid leaking from the batteries had killed the bacteria. The condition of the *Alvin* showed that this was not the case. Nor could he find anything else that might account for the preservation of the food.

Then he devised an experiment. Bacteria were collected from shallow water near Woods Hole, from the deep sea, and from pure strains of bacteria. The different bacteria were placed in jars with food on which they would live and multiply. The bottles were sealed with rubber caps in which narrow slits were cut. The slits would open under the pressure of deep water, and allow the water in.

Half the bottles were taken out to sea. They were lowered to various depths and attached to lines holding a moored buoy. Identical bottles, with identical bacteria, were kept in the laboratory refrigerator. They were at the exact same temperature as the bottles at sea.

Dr. Jannasch recovered and opened individual bottles from the shore and the sea after periods of two, four and six months. He compared bottles from the sea with bottles from the laboratory refrigerator. In each case, he found much less bacterial growth and decomposition in the sea bottle than in the identical shore bottle. In fact, the sea bottles showed between 1/10 and 1/600 the amount of bacterial activity found in the laboratory bottles.

What does this mean?

M. Berger

One of Dr. Jannasch's co-workers examines material that
had been in the ocean for six months.

The experiment shows that the ocean is not such a good place to dump sewage and garbage. The bacteria, it seems, are not nearly as active in deep sea water as they are in soil or in sewage treatment plants.

Some scientists have read these reports and refuse to be alarmed. It may be one hundred or one thousand years before the oceans are ruined, they say.

But Dr. Jannasch believes that if we know we are fouling the ocean, no matter how slowly, we should stop immediately.

The future of the oceans—indeed, the future of all mankind—may depend on what the people of the world do with Dr. Jannasch's startling findings.

BIOLOGISTS

The marine biologists study life in the sea. And they have a most wonderful subject for study. The seas are teeming with both plants and animals.

The largest number of living beings in the sea are classified as plankton. Plankton includes thousands of different types of tiny sea plants and animals. The name comes from the Greek word that means to drift or wander. The many microscopic plankton organisms are moved helplessly about by the ocean tides and currents.

All animal life in the sea depends on plankton. Some fish eat plankton directly. Others eat smaller sea creatures that have eaten plankton.

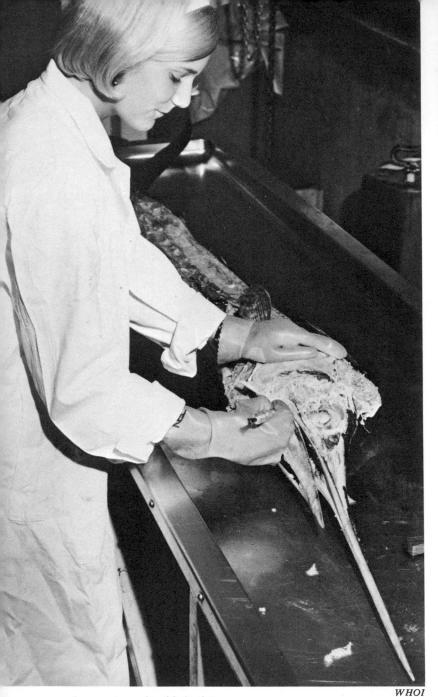

WHOI

A young marine biologist dissects a rather unattractive swordfish.

The oceanographer prepares a plankton net to be towed through the water.

WHOI

WHOI

*Lowering a plankton net
into the water.
The plankton is collected
in the glass bottle
at the end of the net.*

Biologists follow many different research projects to learn about plankton. They pull very fine nets through the water to collect plankton for study in their laboratories. The biologist going out for a cruise on the *Knorr* used a laser beam to gather more information on plankton in the water.

In one interesting study, biologists are investigating the effect of sewage on plankton growth. For this experiment, the scientists pump a mixture of sea water and sewage through large glass jars containing plankton. From time to time they examine the plankton through a microscope to check their rate of growth. They also test to determine whether the plankton has picked up any poisons from the sewage.

If these experiments are successful, they may bring several benefits to man. They might help him to rid the oceans of sewage pollution. And they might provide more plankton for fish to eat, which, in turn, will provide more food for humans.

Various types of seaweed are also being grown in the water and sewage mixture. Here again the hope is to find a way to clean up sewage-laden water, and to increase the human food supply at the same time.

Biologists concerned with food from the sea are also examining the present methods of fishing. Compared to the way we obtain meat, our system of fishing is terribly old-fashioned. It is as though we still went to the forest and hunted wild animals with bow and arrow.

Experiments are now going on with fish farming. Scientists grow the fish under special conditions in areas where the fish are protected from their natural enemies. And they are devising better ways to capture the fish after they are grown.

NMFS

The scientist is placing microscopic oyster eggs
in the numbered containers.

Hundreds of tiny oyster spats on an empty oyster shell.
Each spat has a diameter of 1/75 of an inch.

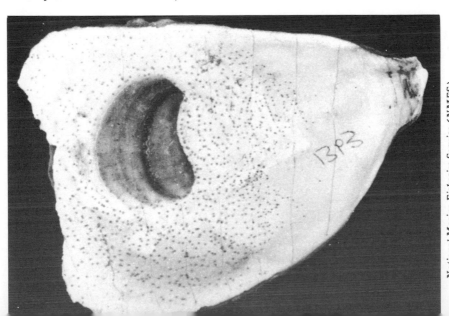

National Marine Fisheries Service (NMFS)

Starfish attacking a bed of oysters.
They pry the shells apart and eat the oysters.

NMFS

Biologists have been particularly successful in raising "crops" of oysters. They start with oyster eggs, which are about 1/5000 of an inch long. The egg is grown under carefully controlled conditions in the lab. When it reaches a size of about 1/75 of an inch, the egg, called a spat, is ready to attach itself to some surface under the water. In the labs, empty oyster shells are used as the surface for the spats. The shells with the spats on them are put in net bags and placed in salt water tanks while the spats develop into mature oysters.

When the oyster is about nine months old it is transplanted to the ocean. In another four or five years the full-grown oyster is ready to be harvested.

Scientists have been experimenting with every step of this process. Different natural foods for the developing oyster are tried. The results of different water temperature, salinity and other factors are studied.

Several particularly helpful suggestions for protecting the oyster from its enemies have come out of these studies. It is estimated that 99 percent of one-month-old oysters are destroyed by enemies —mostly the starfish and the oyster drill, a type of sea snail. Chemicals, such as quicklime, which are applied over oyster beds, kill the enemies without harming the oysters. With the use of quicklime, and other sea-farming methods, 25 percent of the young oysters now survive.

The biologist swings a net over the side of the ship. It is in a frame that will allow it to be dragged along the ocean floor.

WHOI

In the early 1960s it looked as if the American oyster was on its way to becoming extinct. But now marine biologists have reversed this trend, and are producing bumper crops of oysters.

The biologists are interested in every kind of life found in the sea. They put metal tags on large fish, such as the tuna and marlin, to follow their migration patterns. They observe and collect samples of plant and animal life on the ocean floor. They trace the evolution of different types of sea animals.

Anything from the sea that is alive, or that was once alive, is a subject for research by today's marine biologists.

DRIFTING CONTINENTS

Look at a map of the world. Imagine that the Atlantic Ocean is no longer there, and that North and South America and Europe and Africa are moved together.

Do you see how well they fit? Newfoundland goes into the space just above England. The bulge of Africa fits into the Caribbean Sea. And Brazil hugs the coast of Africa beneath the bulge.

For a long time people have wondered about this. Is it a coincidence? Or were the continents all together at one time—and then split apart?

Today, most oceanographers believe that the continents were once joined and that they have been slowly moving, or drifting,

270 Million Years Ago
①
NORTH AMERICA
EUROPE
AFRICA
SOUTH AMERICA

200 Million Years Ago
②
NORTH AMERICA
EUROPE
AFRICA
SOUTH AMERICA

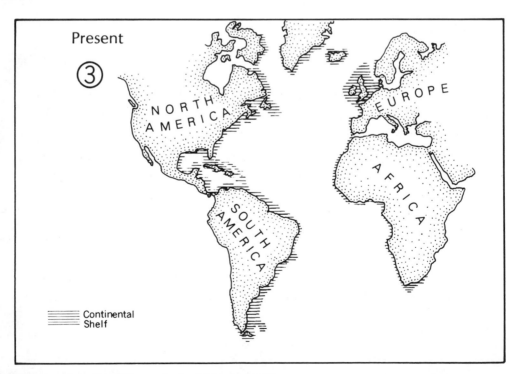

Present
③
NORTH AMERICA
EUROPE
AFRICA
SOUTH AMERICA

Continental Shelf

The continents millions of years ago and today.

apart. Dr. William A. Berggren of the Institution is a leading student of the theory of drifting continents.

Alone, and with others, he has collected fossils of sea animals that lived between 14 and 70 million years ago. He discovered that the fossils from the Mediterranean Sea around North Africa are very similar to those from the Caribbean Sea around Colombia and Venezuela.

He also collected fossils from later periods in those same areas. He found little similarity between the Mediterranean and Caribbean samples of fossils from within the last few million years.

Dr. Berggren explains why the older fossils are similar and the newer fossils are different in this way: millions of years ago North America and Europe were close together. All members of any single species living during that period were alike. Their fossils are similar.

Then the continents began to drift apart. The species were separated. Some stayed on one continent; some on the other. Over a long period of time, differences developed between the two branches of the same species. Fossils of animals that lived after the continents separated are not the same.

In 1970, Dr. Berggren was on a cruise with scientists from other oceanography laboratories. Their purpose was to drill holes deep into the bedrock beneath the Atlantic Ocean.

The rock samples they collected were found to be no more than 200 million years old. Yet, it is known that the planet earth is about 4,600 million years old. And rocks found on the continents are as much as 3,500 million years old.

Why are the rocks under the Atlantic Ocean only 200 million years old?

Dr. Berggren believes that the Atlantic Ocean was not formed until long after the continents came into being. The land on both sides of the Atlantic was once joined together in one supercontinent. Then, about 200 million years ago, Europe and Africa began drifting to the east. And the Atlantic Ocean was created. (The changes in the sea life did not appear until many millions of years after the continents began moving apart.)

Oceanographers have collected other evidence of continental drift. There is a gigantic underwater range of mountains running down the center of the Atlantic Ocean.

Oceanographers have collected samples of rocks from near these mountains. They found that the rocks were formed about one million years ago.

They also collected similar rocks at various distances from the mountains. They found that the farther away the rocks are found, the older they are. The oldest rocks of this type were found at the greatest distances. They were about 140 million years old.

From these findings came the theory that the ocean floor is spreading, that the bottom of the ocean is moving out and away from the central mountain range. It is as though the mountain range is a volcano. Rocks come up through the center and push the continents apart. Scientists estimate that the Atlantic Ocean is growing an inch wider every year.

The shape of the continents, the fossils, the age of the rocks, and the spreading ocean floor, all confirm the theory of drifting continents. No one has put forth any evidence to disprove the theory. Therefore, most oceanographers now accept the idea that the immense continents, moved by forces from deep within the earth, are slowly drifting about on the face of our planet.

GEOLOGISTS

Every few minutes a big wave smashes across the bow of the ship. It sends a chilling spray of salt water over the scientist struggling with his task—connecting long lengths of pipes. One after another, he screws the heavy pipes together. Every so often the ship lurches in the rough seas, making his job that much harder.

Finally, several sections of pipe are joined into one long pipe. At one end he attaches a heavy metal weight.

The entire assembly is called a corer. It will be used to remove a long narrow core of mud from the ocean bottom.

The scientist strains to hook the corer to a cable coming from the winch on the deck. The cable is attached to a giant spool of

A scientist assembling a corer on the deck of the ship.

wire kept beneath the deck. About five miles of wire are wound up on this spool.

He drops the corer over the rail of the ship. The winch motor lowers the corer through the water. It may take up to five hours to lower the corer to the ocean bottom.

The scientist can stop now and rest as the corer is going down. He is wet with perspiration from his efforts to assemble the corer.

The scientist is a geologist. He studies the structure and shape of the ocean floor, and the rocks and mud that are found there.

As soon as a part of the corer touches bottom, a trigger releases the metal weight. The weight drives the hollow tube straight down through the soft mud. A typical corer digs about 20 feet down into the mud.

The corer goes over the side
with a big splash.

U.S. Naval Oceanographic Office

U.S. Naval Oceanographic Office

*Two oceanographers examine the layers of mud in a core
that has just been brought up from the bottom.*

M. Berger

After studying the cores,
the geologist prepares charts
that show the content of each layer.

Cores in plastic tubes await study
in the geologist's laboratory.

M. Berger

This mud on the ocean bottom is called sediment. It has been slowly piling up on the ocean floor since the birth of the ocean. There are many separate layers in the sediment—soil and pebbles brought by rivers emptying into the sea, dust and ashes from exploding volcanoes, and sand blown from deserts by powerful wind storms. Remains of dead marine life also add to the sediment. Large quantities of tiny plankton shells are found here.

When the corer is filled with sediment, it stops. Metal leaves across the bottom prevent the mud from slipping out. The geologist uses the winch to haul the corer up to the ship.

The scientist pushes the long, round core of mud out of the metal pipe. He examines each of the separate layers. He can read the layers in the core the way you can read the pages in a book. He can tell where they came from, when they became part of the sediment, and the water conditions at that time. To the geologist, the core is both a science book and a history book.

After examining it quickly on deck, the geologist usually wraps the long core in plastic so he can study it more carefully in his laboratory.

Sometimes the geologist is interested only in the mud, rocks, plants and animals lying on the top of the sediment. In these cases, he lowers a tool, called a grab, over the side of the ship. When the grab reaches the bottom, the hollow jaws come together and scoop up a sample of the top layer.

For their studies of the ocean bottom, the geologists use underwater cameras. The camera is of a special design. It is attached to

The orange-peel grab is lowered to scoop up a sample of the top layer of bottom mud. This is called an orange-peel grab because of the shape of the jaws.

WHOI

WHOI

The underwater camera and lights are mounted on a frame to be lowered to the ocean bottom.

A photograph of the plants and rocks on the ocean bottom.

WHOI

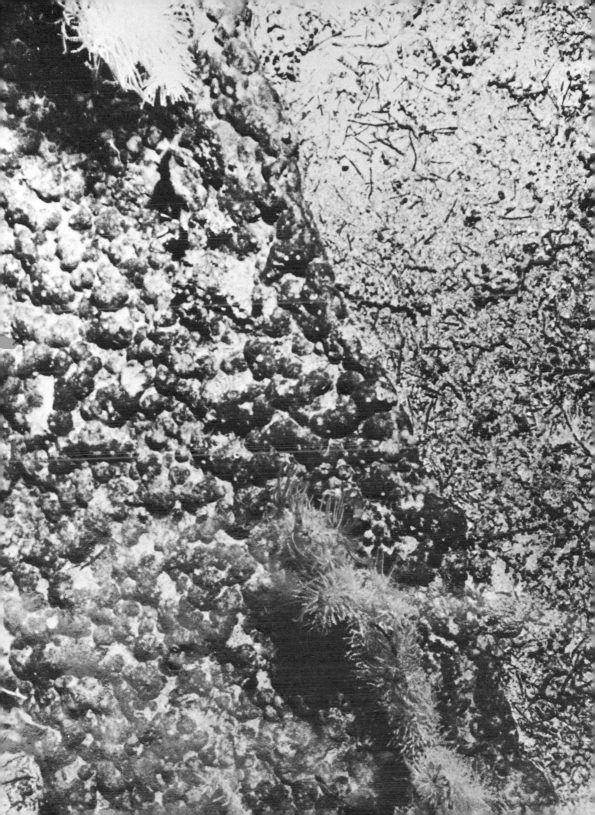

several very bright lights that will illuminate the dark ocean floor. A heavy weight hangs from beneath the camera. As soon as the weight touches the bottom it automatically flashes the lights and takes a picture.

Elizabeth T. Bunce, one of the scientists in the geology department, is most interested in the over-all shape of the ocean floor. She wants to learn about the mountains, valleys and ridges that crisscross the bottom of the sea.

Miss Bunce, and the other geologists, have several tools that use sound to map the ocean bottom. An electrical "pinger" attached to the hull or an air gun or electrical sparker towed along

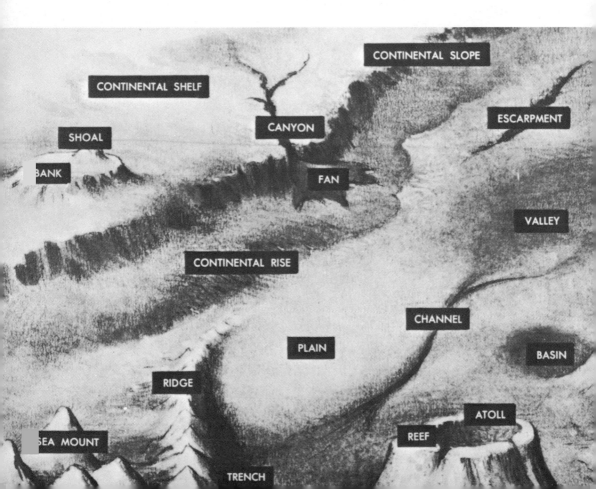

behind the ship can make sounds every few seconds. Sometimes the geologist will explode a half pound of TNT in the water as the sound source.

The sound waves travel off in all directions through the water. Some go down to the ocean bottom. When they strike bottom, the sound waves bounce off and head back up, like echoes.

Hydrophones, a type of microphone, pick up the reflected sound. Automatic equipment measures the time between the original sound and the return of the echo. From this measurement the machine is able to calculate the depth of the water at that point.

The results may be in the form of a chart showing a profile

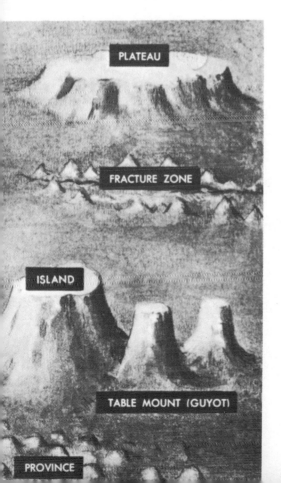

A drawing of the geological features beneath the sea.

U.S. Naval Oceanographic Office

85

picture of the ocean bottom. Or they may appear as a list of numbers on a long strip of paper.

Sound is also the best way to communicate underwater. Other methods of communication, such as radio or light signals, do not work well in water. Geologists do research on underwater sounds. They perform experiments to learn how sounds are changed by different conditions in the water and how underwater communication can be improved.

Some geologists use very sensitive instruments to measure gravity and the earth's magnetism. Their results have given a more complete picture of the geology of the oceans. Some areas produce unexpected results. These places are investigated further by taking up cores or by using echoes to map the ocean bottom.

Surrounding every continent is a narrow ledge. It is called the continental shelf. For many years the geologists at the Institution have been doing a special study of the continental shelf that extends into the Atlantic Ocean along the eastern coast of the United States.

The geologists want to draw accurate and complete maps of the shelf. They want to know what materials make up the shelf and how and when it was formed.

The practical subject of obtaining minerals from the sea and from beneath the sea is another subject for the geologists' research. They are particularly interested in the metal rocks, or nodules, which are found in great numbers on the ocean floor. The nodules are rich in a rare and valuable metal, manganese. In some parts of

The explosion of a half-pound
of TNT sends a fountain of water
up into the air.
Geologists measure the time
between the explosion
and the echo off the bottom to
calculate the water depth.

the Pacific Ocean there are over 100,000 tons of manganese lying on each square mile of ocean bottom.

The most valuable mineral product now coming from the sea— really from beneath the sea—is oil. Obtaining oil from under the sea is a mixed blessing. Offshore oil wells now provide about one quarter of the world's supply. But leaks at the oil wells and accidents to ships carrying oil are polluting the ocean. Millions of gallons of oil spill into the sea every year. Marine chemists now are seeking ways to protect the oceans against the dangers of oil pollution.

The heavy-chain dredge is used to collect rock samples from the ocean bottom.

WHOI

OIL POLLUTION

Early in the morning of September 16, 1969, the oil barge *Florida* broke free of her lines. She smashed ashore at West Falmouth, Cape Cod, just a few miles from Woods Hole. The impact split open her steel hull. About 65,000 gallons of fuel oil poured into the water.

The next day, scientists from nearby Woods Hole went to the scene of the disaster. These researchers had decided to use this opportunity to do a detailed study of oil pollution. They wanted to study its effects on the sea and on life in the sea.

They were shocked by what they saw. The water was the color of coffee, brown and thick. The beach was soaked with dark and smelly oil. Many dead and dying fish, crabs, lobsters and sea worms lay scattered on the sand. Among them, too, lay a number of dead birds, their feathers coated with the sticky oil.

A few days later scientists used nets to collect fish, shellfish and worms from the water. To their dismay they found that about 95 percent of the sea animals they brought in were already dead. The other 5 percent were dying.

Then they brought up samples of the sediment from the area. They found that the oil had soaked deep into the bottom mud. The samples that the scientists collected included many plants and animals from the bottom of the sea. They, too, had been killed by the oil.

Dr. Max Blumer, of the Institution's chemistry department, was one of the scientists most interested in learning more about the oil spill. Dr. Blumer is an organic chemist. Organic chemistry is the study of all compounds that contain carbon atoms.

For many years, Dr. Blumer has been working to increase science's understanding of organic compounds in the sea. He has done research on the sources and quantities of the organic compounds found in the sea, their effect on sea life, how long they remain in the water, and how they can be removed.

Dr. Blumer has been particularly interested in the hydrocarbons, the organic compounds containing only carbon and hydrogen atoms. Recent experiments had convinced him that once a hydrocarbon entered the water, it stayed there for a long time.

He was able to trace one particular hydrocarbon from sea water, to the plankton that picked it up from the water, to shellfish and herrings and sharks that got it from the plankton. The hydrocarbon compound stayed the same as it went through this food chain.

The hydrocarbon that Dr. Blumer traced is harmless. But some of the hydrocarbons found in oil are poisonous, and some are suspected to be causes of cancer. What if these compounds entered the food chain? What if they were in the fish that human beings eat?

Scientists from Woods Hole set up test stations in the area of the oil spill. They wanted to observe the oil pollution over a period of time. Would the oil be broken down and drift away? Would it be taken in by the plants and animals and remain in the area?

Chemical tests of the water went on for over a year. The results showed that sea bacteria did break down some parts of the oil. But these parts of the oil were not poisonous or cancer-causing. The oil that remained was even more concentrated and more poisonous.

In one experiment, some shellfish were removed from the site of the pollution and placed in clean water. After six months these fish still contained the poisons and were unfit to eat.

Dr. Blumer estimates that there are about 10,000 oil spills each year. There are the accidents at the large number of offshore oil wells, spills from the tankers and barges carrying oil throughout the world, and leaks from the ships that use oil for fuel and lubrication. At least five million tons of oil get into the oceans every year. And the actual figure may be as much as one hundred times higher.

Everyone knows of the immediate results of oil pollution. Life in the sea is killed, many sea birds die, and the beaches are ruined. But scientists, such as Dr. Blumer, are also worried about the long-term results. They know that some sea animals communicate by sending and receiving tiny bits of chemical substances through the water. Oil in the water throws off this natural activity. Pollution may lead to the disappearance of certain types of marine life.

An aerial view of oil spreading out from a leaking
offshore oil well. The barge at the bottom of the photo has
a pipe going to the well to try to control
the pouring out of the oil.

Environmental Protection Agency

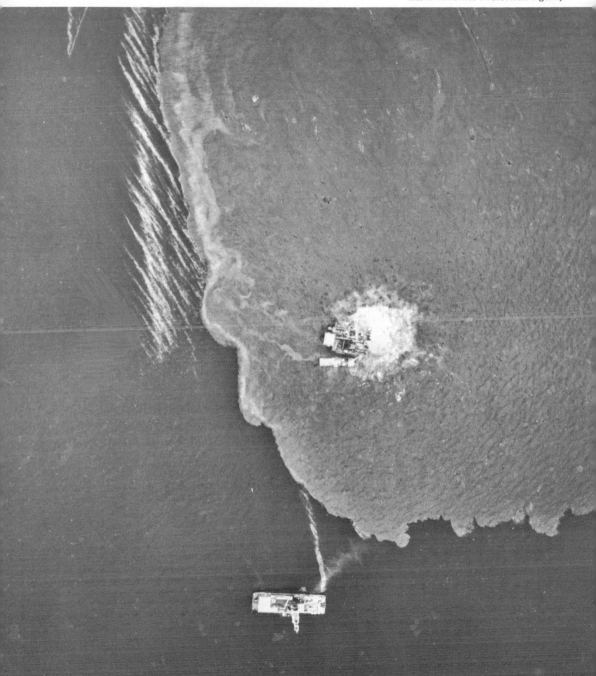

A giant oil well
structure off the coast
of Louisiana.
It includes living
quarters for
forty-three men.

Robert Yarnall Richie—Texaco

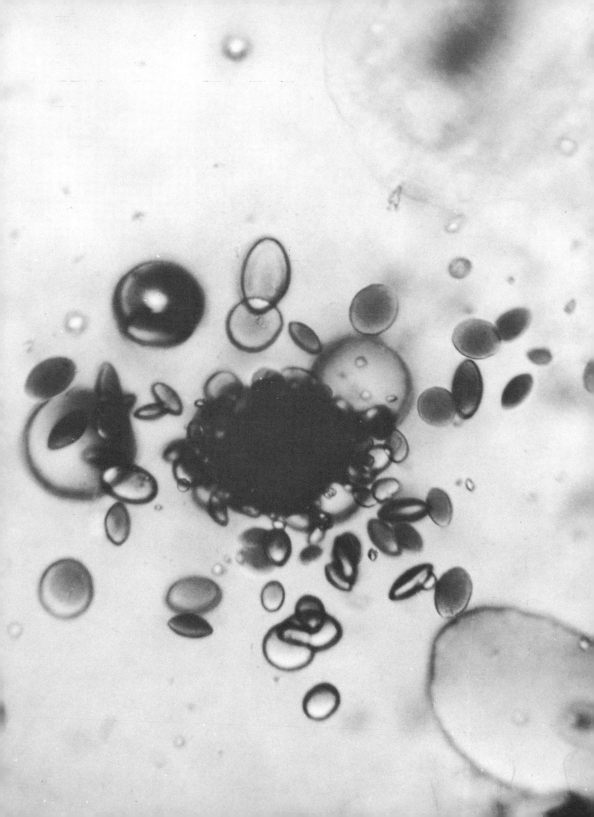

The poisonous and cancer-causing compounds found in oil may, sooner or later, appear in the fish man eats. In time we may not be able to eat any food taken from the sea.

Research is the way to control oil pollution. Scientists must learn all they can about the unspoiled state of the ocean. Then they must discover the exact changes caused by pollution. They must help oil drillers, oil transporters and oil users to prevent oil spills and leaks. And they must develop good, safe methods of cleaning up any oil that does get into the sea.

Oil pollution is an urgent problem. It cannot be put off, to be solved some day in the future. Our use and enjoyment of the ocean—for food, recreation, travel—depend on the research of Dr. Blumer and the other chemists who are struggling to understand and control oil pollution.

This photograph,
taken through a microscope,
shows the results of an experiment
in which bacteria are used
to get rid of oil.
Each oval is a colony of
more than a million bacteria.

U.S. Naval Oceanographic Office

CHEMISTS

The scientist climbs out onto a tiny platform that extends out from the side of the research ship. He leans against the chain railing to keep from slipping off his precarious perch. From this dangerous position he directs the lowering of the steel wire from the winch. At certain points along the wire he attaches 20-inch-long bronze metal tubes.

The tubes are called Nansen bottles. They are used to collect water samples at various depths. The scientist using the Nansen bottles is a marine chemist, studying the chemistry of the sea water.

When the entire length of wire is over the side, the chemist drops a doughnut-shaped weight down the wire. As it falls, it trips

each of the Nansen bottles. One after another, the bottles flip over
and trap about one and one-half quarts of water.

As the wire is brought back up, the chemist takes off the Nansen
bottles. He places them in racks built into the wall of his ship
laboratory. To identify the chemicals in the water, he may pour

*The Nansen bottles, with their valuable water samples,
are kept in racks in the ship's laboratories.*

WHOI

part of each sample into an instrument that automatically analyzes the water. For special measurements he may put the water through various tests in apparatus that he himself assembled.

Sometimes the chemist is looking for chemicals in the water that may be present only in tiny quantities. In these cases, the Nansen bottle does not contain enough water for the chemist to run the necessary tests. He uses containers that hold many gallons to collect bigger samples.

In still another method he collects water as the ship is steaming along. He hangs a pipe over the side and uses a pump to draw up the water. It then flows through the testing equipment and goes back over the side.

All of the chemical elements known to man are found in sea water, and all of these chemicals are of interest to the marine chemists. There are, though, a few chemicals of particular concern. He studies the oxygen in the water because life in the sea depends on the amount of oxygen dissolved in the water. He studies the radioactive elements in the sea, and how they affect life there.

One of the chemist's major concerns is the salinity of sea water. He knows that the rivers bring the salt into the ocean. The rivers wash out the salt compounds from the land through which they pass. As the rivers flow into the sea, they carry along the salt, making the sea water salty.

The scientists find remarkably little variation in the salinity in the oceans of the world. It is always around 3.5 percent. The percentage does differ slightly, though, from place to place. In the Arctic Ocean it is only 3.3 percent. In the Persian Gulf there is 4.0 percent salt content.

*The marine chemist stands on a tiny perch as
he brings in a large container of water.*

WHOI

Over the years several ships have left the docks at Woods Hole to head for the Black Sea, which is located at the eastern end of the Mediterranean, between Russia and Turkey. It is one of the fascinating places for research. The surface waters of the Black Sea are normal. But beneath a depth of about 300 feet there is very little oxygen in the water. Hardly any forms of life can be found below that level.

Many scientists are trying to learn more about the strange chemistry of the Black Sea. Chemists from the Institution are particularly interested in the border between the oxygen and the non-oxygen, between life and absence of life.

But not all of the chemists at the Institution collect and study samples of water from the sea. Some spend most of their time doing experiments in their shore labs. One major group of experiments is exploring how sea animals communicate—especially how they use chemicals to communicate.

The chemists have evidence that chemical messengers are sent and received through the water to help sea animals find food, avoid enemies, organize into large groups and to find mates.

Chemists at Woods Hole have done some dramatic experiments to learn more about chemical underwater communication. In a recent experiment, a chemist placed a starfish at one end of a long narrow tank filled with sea water. At the opposite end he placed an oyster—a favorite food of the starfish.

Within seconds, he saw the starfish begin to move down the tank, heading straight for the oyster. In a few minutes, the starfish clambered over the oyster. He forced open the oyster shell and ate the oyster.

These large containers of water
were brought back to the shore laboratory
for careful study.

WHOI

The starfish senses the presence of an oyster in the same tank and immediately attacks the unlucky oyster.

Marine chemists believe that the oyster releases some chemical substance into the water. The starfish recognizes either the taste or smell, even at great distances. Once he senses the substance, the starfish heads toward the source—and the unlucky oyster.

NMFS

   The chemists have found evidence of chemical communication in several different types of sea creatures. Some of these chemicals have already been isolated and identified. But there is still a long way to go before chemical communication and the chemistry in the sea is fully understood.

PHYSICAL OCEANOGRAPHERS

Alongside the rail of the research ship is a small wooden rack. Lying on it is a rusty-looking metal device. It looks like a small bomb—a long, narrow tube coming to a point at one end, with fins at the other end.

A scientist comes over to the rack. He slides a small rectangle of dark glass into the body of the device. Then he hooks the front end to a wire cable and lowers it into the water to be towed as the ship steams along.

This scientist is using one of the oldest and most reliable tools of the oceanographers. They call it a BT. The full name is the bathythermograph.

The BT measures both the temperature and the pressure of the water through which it is towed. One side of the glass that the scientist inserted is coated with black carbon. A sharp needle rests against this side of the glass. The needle is moved by changes in the temperature and pressure of the water. It scratches a line in the carbon coating of the glass.

When the oceanographer recovers the BT, he removes the glass. The line in the carbon gives him a permanent record of the temperature and pressure of the water through which the BT was towed.

The BT is one of the most popular tools of the physical oceanographers. Physical oceanographers study the currents and waves of the ocean. They seek to understand the movements and actions of the water.

Ocean currents are streams of water flowing within the water of the ocean. They are sometimes described as rivers passing through the ocean. The currents are created by the action of the winds and the earth's rotation on the ocean water.

The Gulf Stream is a very big and very powerful system of currents. It begins in the Gulf of Mexico and moves up the eastern coast of the United States. Then it heads east across the Atlantic Ocean toward Europe, where it splits into several smaller currents.

Christopher Columbus, in September 1492, was the first to mention this current. Some years later, in 1513, Ponce de Leon claimed that this current drove his ships backwards. In 1768 Benjamin Franklin noted that the current seemed to start in the Gulf of Mexico. He named it the Gulf Stream.

For many years the physical oceanographers at Woods Hole have been conducting a very special study of the Gulf Stream.

The BT, which just measured
the temperature and pressure of
the water, is hauled up.

The glass slide the scientist
removed from the BT.
The wavy line shows the temperature
and pressure of the water.

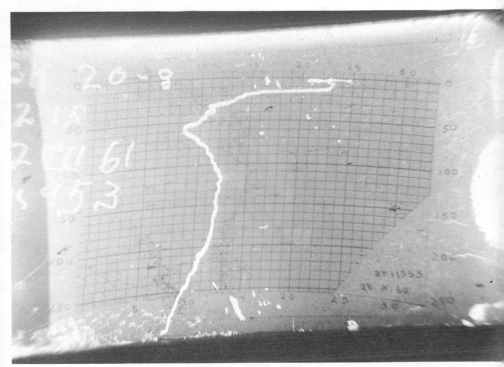

WHOI

WHOI

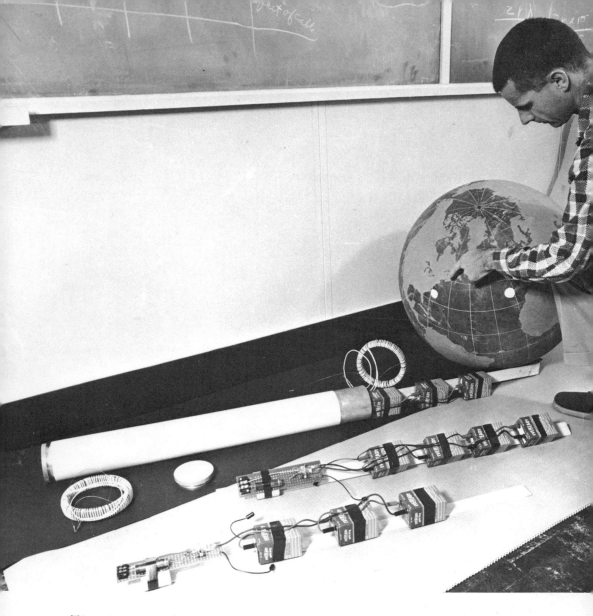

They have used a variety of tools and methods to learn more about the Gulf Stream, and other ocean currents as well.

One way to trace the path of a current is to throw an object into the water and see where it is carried by the current. Every

Views inside a float,
showing the batteries and pinger.
The oceanographer is tracing the path of a float
on the globe.

WHOI

year the physical oceanographers at the Institution drop thousands of drift bottles into the water from research ships.

The scientist first places some sand in the bottle, usually an empty soda pop bottle. This makes the bottle heavier so it will float just below the surface of the water. In this way the bottle is moved only by the current, and not by the wind.

The physical oceanographer also places a card inside each bottle, which is then tightly sealed with a cork and thrown into the water. The card asks the person finding the bottle to write where and when the bottle was found, and to mail the card back to Woods Hole. A reward of 50 cents is offered to anyone who returns a card with the information.

About 10,000 bottles are dropped into the sea every year. About 1,000 cards are returned. One year a card was returned with a bullet hole through it. A note explained that the finder could not remove the bottle cork. So he shot it open with his pistol. Another finder brought the bottle to the Institution in person. He insisted on a reward of $5.00. He was refused.

The physical oceanographers chuckle most over the card that came back with a bill for $27.95. A young man found the bottle on a public beach in New Jersey. A girl watched him bring it in. They became friendly, and he invited her out for dinner. The meal cost him $27.95, but he decided that he did not like the girl. Since it was all caused by the drift bottle, he wanted his money back from the Institution.

Drift bottles show the movement of the surface current. But scientists also want to know what is happening beneath the surface. To trace the underwater currents they use various kinds of floats.

The usual float is a long metal tube. Weights are added so that the float will remain at any desired depth. Inside the float a battery-powered sounder sends out loud "pings," that can be heard from great distances.

The float is thrown over the side of the research ship. Directional hydrophones on the ship pick up the sounds from the float. The ship is then able to follow the path of the float, and therefore, of the current. It is the same as hanging a bell on a cat. You can follow the cat by listening for the bell.

Physical oceanographers also use tools and instruments that are kept in one place in the ocean. They often attach these devices to floating buoys that are anchored or moored to remain in one spot.

One popular buoy looks like a bright red doughnut, with a steel tower above. Beneath is a long cable going down to an anchor on the sea floor. The scientist can place his instruments on the buoy itself or at any point along the cable.

On the tower he often places weather instruments, to measure the wind and the temperature. The weather plays a big part in shaping the currents. Knowing the weather helps to understand the current.

On the cable the scientist attaches different measuring tools. The flowmeter measures the speed and direction of the current. It has blades like a propeller and a vane like a weather vane. The spinning of the blades is a measure of the water speed. And the vane causes the flowmeter to face in the direction of the current. A combined tool makes three different measurements all at once. It electrically measures the saltiness, the temperature and the pressure of the water.

Usually there is a battery-operated radio on the buoy. The measurements are broadcast every six hours. They are received either at Woods Hole or on one of the research ships.

Scientists struggle and strain to launch a buoy
when the seas are rough.

A doughnut buoy on the dock.
Some of the instruments on the tower are already in place.

WHOI

M. Bergér

The physical oceanographers have learned a great deal about the Gulf Stream—and other ocean currents—from these studies.

They know that the surface Gulf Stream current is warmer than the water through which it flows. When the Gulf Stream passes near northern Europe it warms the coastal land areas by as much as 15 degrees. There are ports in Norway near the Gulf Stream where men can fish all year. Yet, ports 800 miles farther south are

frozen solid for the winter months—without the warmth from the Gulf Stream.

They have discovered that the Gulf Stream is not a single current. Rather, it is a series of short separate currents, all going roughly in the same direction and at the same temperature and speed. And they have found that underneath the surface Gulf Stream there is another current. This one, though, goes in the

Physical oceanographers built
this fence to study
the wave patterns on a beach.

NOAA

In this 14-foot rotating tank the physical oceanographers can study the theory of ocean currents.

M. Berger

opposite direction, bringing colder water back to the Gulf of Mexico. The physical oceanographers at the Institution have shown that the Gulf Stream is a most complicated system of moving waters.

Not all the physical oceanographers at the Institution go out on

research cruises. Some scientists are more interested in the theory of currents and waves than in observing the ocean itself.

In their shore laboratory these scientists have a large, round tank, about 14 feet in diameter. The tank can spin at speeds up to 20 turns per minute. When it is filled with water, the spinning

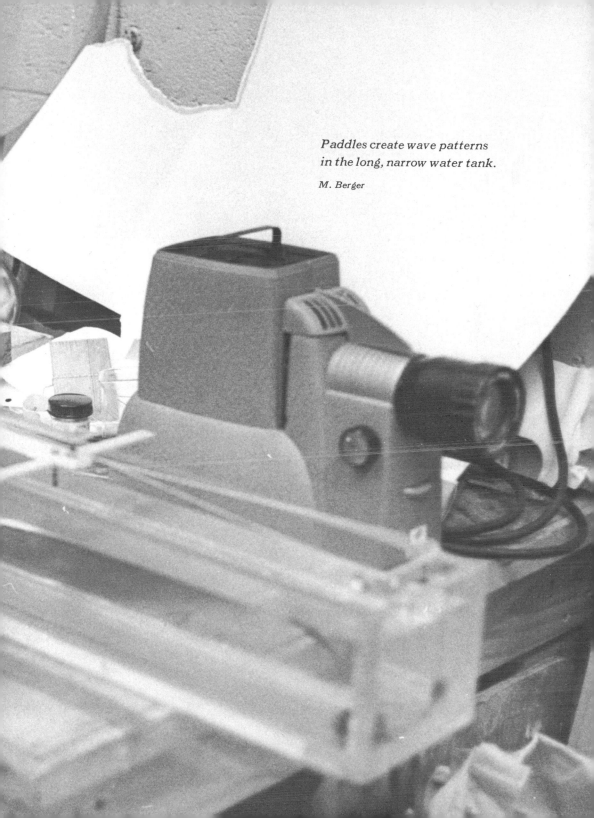

Paddles create wave patterns
in the long, narrow water tank.

M. Berger

moves the water somewhat like the earth's rotation moves the oceans.

The scientists add colored dyes to the water, build obstructions in the tank, and spin the tank at different speeds. Through their work they are slowly coming to a basic understanding of the theory of ocean currents.

In this laboratory there is also a long, narrow tank. Metal paddles hang over this tank. They are used to create different wave patterns in the water. The scientists perform experiments on how waves are reflected back and forth, what happens when waves collide, and so on.

The physical oceanographer, whether observing the ocean from a research ship or doing experiments in a laboratory, is learning more about the physical forces at work in the ocean. Together with the marine biologists, geologists and chemists he, or she, is advancing the science of oceanography:

—increasing our basic knowledge of the sea,

—controlling pollution,

—discovering new food, mineral and energy sources.

These dedicated men and women have made oceanography one of the most important and most dynamic of the modern sciences.

FURTHER READING

Introductory books on oceanography:

ADLER, IRVING and RUTH, *Oceans*, New York, John Day, 1962.
ARNOV, BORIS, *Oceans of the World*, Indianapolis, Bobbs-Merrill, 1962.
COMBS, CHARLES, *Deep-sea World*, New York, William Morrow, 1966.
SHERMAN, DIANE, *You and the Oceans*, Chicago, Childrens Press, 1965.

More advanced books on oceanography:

BEHRMAN, DANIEL, *The New World of the Oceans*, Boston, Little Brown, 1969.
BRIGGS, PETER, *Men in the Sea*, New York, Simon and Schuster, 1968.

GABER, NORMAN H., *Your Future in Oceanography,* New York, Richards Rosen, 1967.

STEPHENS, WILLIAM M., *Science Beneath the Sea,* New York, Putnam, 1966.

YASSO, WARREN E., *Oceanography,* New York, Holt, Rinehart, Winston, 1965.

INDEX

DENNIS STRATTON CREMIN MEMORIAL
GAVIN NORTH SCHOOL
LAKE VILLA, ILLINOIS   60046

ABOUT THE AUTHOR

Melvin Berger was born in New York City. He was educated at City College; University of Rochester, where he received his Bachelor's Degree; Columbia University, where he earned his Master's Degree; and London University.

Mr. Berger loves to travel and it was during his travels that he made many side visits to laboratories. The idea for the series "Scientists at Work" grew out of these visits.

Mr. Berger lives with his wife and two daughters on Long Island, New York.

SCIENTISTS AT WORK